For Ernesto, Aaron, and Teddy —P. B.

For Ashleigh Rae and Samson Gregory —D. J. O.

Farrar Straus Giroux Books for Young Readers
An imprint of Macmillan Publishing Group, LLC
120 Broadway, New York, NY 10271 • mackids.com

Text copyright © 2024 by Phil Bildner.
Illustrations copyright © 2024 by Daniel J. O'Brien.
All rights reserved.

Our books may be purchased in bulk for promotional, educational, or business use.
Please contact your local bookseller or the Macmillan Corporate and Premium Sales Department
at (800) 221-7945 ext. 5442 or by email at MacmillanSpecialMarkets@macmillan.com.

Library of Congress Control Number: 2023937540

First edition, 2024
Designed by Mike Burroughs. Production was supervised by Celeste Cass,
and the production editor was Ilana Worrell. Edited by Wesley Adams and Hannah Miller.
Color separations by Embassy Graphics
Printed in China by RR Donnelley Asia Printing Solutions Ltd., Dongguan City, Guangdong Province

ISBN 978-0-374-39122-5

10 9 8 7 6 5 4 3 2 1

GLENN BURKE, GAME CHANGER

The Man Who Invented the High Five

PHIL BILDNER

ILLUSTRATED BY
DANIEL J. O'BRIEN

Farrar Straus Giroux
New York

On the baseball diamond,
Glenn Burke was a five-tool talent.

ONE!

Glenn flew around the bases.
Ran faster than all the other
neighborhood kids in North Oakland.

TWO!

He always put a bat on the ball.
Sprayed his hits all over
Bushrod Park.

THREE!

He hit with power.
One time, he blasted a home run
out of the park, over Racine Street,
and all the way to Telegraph Avenue.

FOUR!

Glenn had a glove.
He caught everything hit his way—pop-ups,
ground balls, line drives—everything.

FIVE!

Glenn's right arm was a cannon.
One time, he fired a one-bounce missile
from the center-field fence at Diamond Stadium
straight into the catcher's mitt.

OUT!

When Glenn Burke got called up to the big leagues and put on his Dodgers uniform, he caught the attention of the coaches.

Five-tool talents didn't come around that often.

Five-tool talents could change the game.

Glenn Burke caught the attention of his new teammates, too. In the locker room, he danced around and performed comedy routines. At practice, he stuffed towels under his jersey and imitated his manager, Tommy Lasorda. During games, he cheered louder than everyone.

He caught the attention of the fans, too. They loved the energy and excitement he brought to their team. They knew Glenn Burke could be a game changer.

But the fans didn't know he already was changing the game. Glenn Burke was gay. Most of his teammates knew. Or had an idea he was. Most didn't care. It didn't make a difference to them.

But it made a difference to his manager, Tommy Lasorda. Tommy's son was gay, too, and Tommy couldn't stand that he was. When he found out his son was friends with Glenn, he made his son stay away.

Glenn was crushed.

It made a difference to the Dodgers' general manager, too. "Everyone on the team is married but you, Glenn," Al Campanis said. "When players get married on the Dodgers, we help them out financially."

Glenn Burke couldn't believe his ears. The Dodgers were offering to *pay* him to marry a woman. "Al, I have no plans of marrying anyone anytime soon," he said.

It would've made a difference to a lot of people. Back in the 1970s, most gay people *couldn't* live openly. Often, they were fired from their jobs or kicked out of their homes when others learned they were gay. Gay people were frequently bullied and attacked.

Glenn Burke tried to keep his identity a secret. He understood that most people weren't ready for him—or anyone—to make history as the first openly gay Major League Baseball player.

But Glenn Burke was about to make history in a whole other way.

Heading into the last game of Glenn's rookie season, the Dodgers had a chance to do something no team had ever done before. No team ever had four players hit thirty home runs each in the same season. Three players on the Dodgers already had thirty, and a fourth, Dusty Baker, had twenty-nine. The Dodgers were one Dusty Baker home run away from the record books.

On the mound for the opposing team was J. R. Richard, the hardest-throwing fireballer in all of baseball. Dusty didn't hit a home run in his first at bat. He didn't hit a home run in his second at bat either.

Dusty had one last chance.
Ball one. Strike one. Strike two.
Dusty Baker dug in at the plate.
J. R. Richard rocked into his windup.
He fired his fastball.
CRACK!

HOME RUN!

As Dusty Baker trotted around the bases, Glenn Burke bolted from the on-deck circle.

"Way to go!" he shouted. "Way to go!"

When Dusty Baker crossed home plate, Glenn Burke threw his right arm into the air and waved his hand. Dusty Baker smacked Glenn Burke's right hand with his own right hand.

A high five. The first-ever high five.

Next, Glenn Burke stepped into the batter's box.

CRACK!

His very first big-league home run!

When Dusty Baker greeted Glenn on the steps of the dugout, Dusty threw his right arm into the air and waved his hand. Glenn smacked Dusty's right hand with his own right hand. A high five. The second-ever high five.

A handshake was born.

That season, the high-fiving Los Angeles Dodgers made it all the way to the World Series, and in Game One at Yankee Stadium, Glenn Burke started in center field.

But a few months later, Glenn was traded to the Oakland Athletics, one of the worst teams in all of baseball.

The Dodger players were furious. "You traded our best prospect!" one told the general manager. "Not to mention the life of the team!"

Dusty knew why Glenn had been traded. So did most of his teammates. So did Glenn.

He was crushed.

The Athletics didn't want Glenn on their team either. Their manager made that clear. He made sure the other players made it clear, too.

Some of them harassed him. Some of them spat on him. Some of them refused to go near him in the clubhouse.

Glenn got the message. It was time to go.
Baseball wasn't ready to embrace a game changer like him.

But baseball embraced his game-changing handshake.
So did soccer, football, basketball, and hockey. Sports all
around the country and all around the world.

All of a sudden, everyone
everywhere was high-fiving.

After baseball, Glenn Burke found his people. He found a community that welcomed and accepted him for who he was. He starred for the Pendulum Pirates in the San Francisco Gay Softball League. His team voted him Player of the Year.

He played in the Gay Olympics. His team won gold.

Many nights, Glenn would sit on the hood of a parked car in the Castro District and high-five the passersby.

Glenn may have found his people, but he didn't find peace. All those years of pretending to be someone he wasn't and being treated like he wasn't enough simply for being who he was had taken a toll.

It would've taken a toll on almost anyone.

Glenn had trouble holding on to jobs. He had trouble paying his rent. He got into trouble with drugs and the law.

One evening, he got hit by a car. The accident shattered his leg in four places, shattered what was left of his five-tool talents.

Then Glenn tested positive for HIV, the virus that causes AIDS. Back then, there were very few treatments. Back then, it was up to family and friends to care for those who got sick.

Glenn Burke died of AIDS in 1995. He was only forty-two years old.

Luckily, Glenn lived long enough to see his handshake become a universal greeting of joy and jubilation and of energy and excitement.

Our universal greeting.

But he didn't live long enough to see the other part of his legacy, one just as lasting and universal and even more important.

His bravery paved the way for others to live their lives openly and free.

Glenn Burke changed the game.

AUTHOR'S NOTE

Whenever I get the opportunity to talk with young people about writing, I often say that to be a good writer, you have to be willing to listen. You're not always going to like what you hear—you're *definitely* not always going to like what you hear—but you have to be willing to listen.

These days, as an example, I share the origin story of the book you're currently holding, which starts with me sharing the origin story of my middle grade novel *A High Five for Glenn Burke*.

One of my favorite documentary series of the early 2000s was ESPN Films' *30 for 30*, which showcased memorable sports moments, teams, and individuals. In 2014, they released the short film *The High Five*, which told the backstory of our universally known celebratory gesture. I was familiar with some of the history, and after watching the film, I recall thinking: "There's a picture book in here somewhere." But at the time, I was working on other projects, and a picture book—if there was in fact a picture book in there somewhere—would have to wait.

A little over two years later, I returned to the idea. I decided the best approach would be to write the picture book as a biography of Glenn Burke. Many drafts later, I'd completed a manuscript titled *A High Five for Glenn Burke* and sent it to my editor.

My editor didn't see it as a picture book. He envisioned something else—a middle grade novel in which Glenn Burke's story played a part.

I *definitely* didn't like hearing that.

Still, I listened. I started rewriting the nonfiction picture book as a novel, drafted a few sample chapters and an outline, and transformed the manuscript into the story of a baseball-loving twelve-year-old boy who's realizing he's gay.

A High Five for Glenn Burke, the middle grade novel, came out in February 2020, right at the start of the COVID-19 pandemic. Despite the unfortunate timing of the release date, the book did well enough that by the end of the year, I decided to send my editor an updated and reimagined version of the Glenn Burke picture book biography. Within a matter of weeks, we were working on *A High Five for Glenn Burke 2.0*, which soon became *Glenn Burke, Game Changer*—this book with its rather unique, full-circle origin story.

This book is all *about* origin stories: the origin of the high five and the origin of Glenn Burke.

Over the years, some have questioned whether Glenn truly invented the high five. One alternative origin story involved Lamont Sleets Sr., a soldier who served in the Vietnam War, and his son Lamont Sleets Jr., a college basketball player at Murray State University. But that turned out to be an elaborate hoax. Another origin story involved members of the 1978–79 Louisville Cardinals men's basketball team, but their high fives took place well after the one between Glenn Burke and Dusty Baker.

Almost certainly, there's another reason why Glenn Burke didn't always get the credit and recognition he deserved. Glenn Burke was a gay Black man who was run out of Major League Baseball and died from AIDS. That's who invented the high five? Glenn's story isn't exactly a feel-good one with a happily-ever-after ending. It sure helps to explain why others tried to erase him and create alternative histories.

Facts matter. History matters. The truth matters.

These days, thankfully, more and more people are accepting and respectful of everyone's humanity, and most now acknowledge that the high five truly did begin with Glenn Burke.

That includes Major League Baseball.

In June 2022, at their annual Pride Night, the Los Angeles Dodgers celebrated the life of Glenn Burke. More than forty members of Glenn's family attended. His brother Sidney threw out the first pitch. Billy Bean, the senior vice president of diversity, equity, and inclusion; special assistant to the commissioner; and the second openly gay Major League Baseball player, participated in the pregame ceremony. All the Dodgers players, for the first time in the history of the franchise, wore custom-made Pride caps during the game.

Everyone and everything for the real game changer, Glenn Burke.

SELECTED BIBLIOGRAPHY

BOOKS AND PERIODICALS

Glenn Burke and Erik Sherman. *Out at Home: The True Story of Glenn Burke, Baseball's First Openly Gay Player*. New York: Berkley, 2015.

John Fredland. "October 2, 1977: Dusty Baker Hits 30th Homer, Receives First-Ever High-Five from Glenn Burke in Dodgers' Loss to Astros," Society for American Baseball Research (no date). https://sabr.org/gamesproj/game/october-2-1977-dusty-baker-hits-30th-homer-receives -first-ever-high-five-from-glenn-burke-in-dodgers-loss-to-astros/.

Andrew Maraniss. *Singled Out: The True Story of Glenn Burke*. New York: Philomel, 2021.

Scott Miller. "The Dodgers Embrace the Family of a Player They Once Shunned," *New York Times*, Updated June 3, 2022. https://www.nytimes.com/2022/06/02/sports/baseball/glenn-burke-dodgers-pride.html.

Jon Mooallem. "The History and Mystery of the High Five," *ESPN Magazine*, August 8, 2011.

Michael J. Smith. "The Double Life of a Gay Dodger," *Inside Sports*, October 1982.

RADIO, FILMS, AND VIDEOS

Doug Harris and Sean Maddison, directors. *Out: The Glenn Burke Story* (2010). Excerpts available on Doug Harris's YouTube channel, https://www.youtube.com/@DougHarris50/videos.

Doug Harris, interviewed by Kelly McEvers. "The Price Glenn Burke Paid for Coming Out," NPR's *All Things Considered*, May 5, 2013. https://www.npr.org/2013/05/05/181410089/the-price-glenn-burke-paid-for-coming-out.

Michael Jacobs, director. *30 for 30 Shorts: The High Five* (ESPN, 2014). https://www.espn.com/video/clip/_/id/11253247.

TIMELINE OF GLENN BURKE'S LIFE AND LEGACY

November 16, 1952

Glenn is born in Oakland, California.

1960s

Throughout his childhood, Glenn often visits Bushrod Park in North Oakland in order to play baseball and basketball.

1970

During his senior year at Berkeley High School, Glenn leads the basketball team to an undefeated season and is awarded Northern California Player of the Year.

June 11, 1972

Glenn meets with Dodgers scout Ray Perry and accepts the team's offer to sign with the organization and join their Minor League baseball club.

June 26, 1972

Glenn plays in his first professional baseball game for Utah's Ogden Dodgers.

May 16, 1978

Glenn is traded to the Oakland Athletics.

June 4, 1979

Glenn plays his last Major League baseball game with the Oakland A's.

1982

Glenn stars for the Pendulum Pirates softball team. The team wins the Gay World Series. Glenn also plays for the gold-medal-winning basketball and softball teams at the first-ever Gay Games (formerly called the Gay Olympics).

September 1982

Glenn comes out as gay in the magazine *Inside Sports* and during a live television interview with Bryant Gumbel, the then-host of NBC's *The Today Show*.